Handbook for Unwell Mothers

poems by

Jill Crammond

Finishing Line Press
Georgetown, Kentucky

Handbook for
Unwell Mothers

Copyright © 2023 by Jill Crammond
ISBN 979-8-88838-211-0 First Edition
All rights reserved under International and Pan-American Copyright Conventions.
No part of this book may be reproduced in any manner whatsoever without written permission from the publisher, except in the case of brief quotations embodied in critical articles and reviews.

ACKNOWLEDGMENTS

"All the Pretty Mothers" and "How We Finally Made It Out of Oz" in *Fire on Her Tongue: An Anthology of Contemporary Women's Poetry*: Two Sylvias Press
"Still Life Without Gratitude" in *Pidgeonholes*
"Still Life: Ex-Wife Washing Dishes in the Burned House" in *Mom Egg Review*
"The Town Witch Tries to Make Friends" in *Fiolet & Wing: An Anthology of Domestic Fabulist Poetry*
"Our Lady of Dark Mysteries" in *Unbroken Journal*
"When the Dark Things Show Up" in *Tiny Spoon*
"Mary Pays Homage" in *Mother Mary Comes to Me: A Popculture Anthology*: Madville Publishing
"The Fireman's Daughter Extinguishes One More Fire" in *Tinderbox Poetry Journal*

Publisher: Leah Huete de Maines
Editor: Christen Kincaid
Cover Art: "La Volonté," www.manouart.wixsite.com/manou
Author Photo: Sophie Wickham
Cover Design: Elizabeth Maines McCleavy

Order online: www.finishinglinepress.com
also available on amazon.com

Author inquiries and mail orders:
Finishing Line Press
PO Box 1626
Georgetown, Kentucky 40324
USA

Table of Contents

All the Pretty Mothers 1

How We Finally Made It Out of Oz 2

Still Life Without Gratitude 3

Still Life: Ex-Wife Washing Dishes in the Burning House 4

Our Lady of Holy Fire 5

Against Sap and Stick 6

How to Swing a Hammer 7

On Forbidding Certain Words at the Dinner Table 8

Love As Sunfish with Hook in its Eye 10

The Town Witch Tries to Make Friends 11

The House that Jane Built 13

Thirteen Ways of Looking at Home 14

Mary Writes an Ars Poetica 16

Our Lady of Dark Mysteries 18

When the Dark Things Show Up 19

One Doll's Epistle to Discontent 20

Mary Looks at Real Estate 21

Mary Kneels in the Garden 22

Mary Pays Homage 24

The Fireman's Daughter Extinguishes One More Fire 26

Preparedness Checklist for Imminent Death 27

*For all the mothers,
unwell, well, and otherwise,
who have traveled with me on this path,
especially my own.*

All the Pretty Mothers

I don't even want to look at you.
And suddenly I am that mother—
cigarette hanging by a slice of lip
hip thrust into the door jamb,
blood-shot eyes drooping
with the weight of yesterday's mascara.

It is morning in the gingerbread house
and no-one has eaten the children yet.

The pretty mothers, already at the bus stop,
guard their children and gawk,
fall back on well-heeled urban myths:

Their pretty mommy was abducted by aliens.
See? That boy and girl didn't do what they were told.
Their mommy turned into a witch
and now she's going to eat them.

I want these children to eat me
out of house and home.
I have laced the curtains with licorice
replaced the windowpanes with spun sugar
strung twinkle lights hung with gummy bears from the ceiling.

I want to run from this fairy tale in flip flops or shit-kickers
because if you haven't figured it out by now
I am not the mother in sensible shoes.

How We Finally Made It Out of Oz

It was the year of the crumbling castle
tornadoes at every turn.

Our home tumbled
around us, the brick I laid
so carefully
turning to webs of straw
and me with no silver loom to weave
our sorry band of lions, tigers, and bears
into something like a poppy field
or a brick road,
roots swelling beneath mud and gold.

You know how it is when you wake
from a dream, the strain of a banjo
(violin if you're lucky) staining the morning
fooling you into believing the best way out
is to find the eye and hurl yourself into the disaster?

You know the epilogue to the *Wizard of Oz?*
The one no one has ever seen
where the little man turns everyone into zombies
who watch wicked Dorothy slip out of her ruby shoes
roll striped stockings up one pale leg at a time,
follow her down that sticky black tar road?

When the castle showed itself to be nothing
more than a poorly drawn barn
when at last it fell to its clapboard knees,
that's when I packed the children
and myself into a glass valise
and we finally saw the way out.

Still Life Without Gratitude

Ghosts have been turning off the lights.
Wires aren't smoldering or burning inside walls,
but the life is melting out of everyone who lives here.

See Dick practice love as lock down drill.
See Jane draft daily escape plans.

By escape I mean map.
By map I mean
there are fires burning that only a controlled burn can extinguish.

Family as candle wax,
as blackened wicks too short or too long.

We are not bound to thank anyone for their kindness,
but there is a man across town who mowed the lawn once,
another not far from here who cleaned the chimney.
Both will be buried in the family plot.

It scares me to think that I might be replaceable,
but I plan my funeral anyway.

Still Life: Ex-Wife Washing Dishes in the Burning House

Nothing you do makes sense.
You light candles just to blow them out,
ask the dark kitchen for a flashlight.

You dress the children in napkins,
fold their pets into neat triangles,
tuck one white cat in your daughter's lunchbox.

You imagine yourself a widow,
burn the pot roast, fill a flask with ashes
scraped from your dirty oven,
carry them from room to room in a broken vase.

In the empty fireplace,
below the boarded-up chimney
you wash breakfast dishes,

imagine the flames will offer a hand,
suck the very molecules from the water
you spray to forgive the plates their stains.

When the fork tines agree to unite,
and the spoons soften their curves,
you are not surprised to find
your head floating where your feet rest.

Our Lady of Holy Fire

Mary carries candles in her sleeves,
lights strangers' hearts on fire when they aren't looking.

Not spontaneous combustion, but close.

Look into the flame, she says.
You won't burn, she says.

Raise your hand if you would love
to have the locked door of your thoracic cage seared wide open.

Raise your hand if you would love.

O Mother of white wicks and long-handled lighters.
What smoke in our eyes.
What soot in our lungs.

Put another way, there is a woman waiting
outside your door and she wants you
to drink more water, turn off the light when you leave a room.

It is cold outside, below zero between your ribs.
She is not your mother.

Raise your hand if you would refuse help from a predator.
Raise your hand if you recognize a predator,
even with the sun in your eyes.
Where have your hands been?

Here are the real questions:
Are you raising your hand each time you are asked?
Are you your own mother or are you the prey?

If I tell you things, finish my prayer
with my voice rising,
am I still asking you what I don't know, or am I your teacher?

Against Sap and Stick
> *It's a wonder the world keeps its whirling.*
> —Kevin Young

Of course, the mothers. Of course, the kitchens. Long-winded aprons of string theory, of protection, of needing a banana to tell the whole story slant. Of course, wine. Of course, red and glasses and where are my glasses? Of course, a spectacle. Of course, a psychic and a ghost. Of course, they walk into a bar. When mom tells that joke. When everyone laughs. When no one is home. When mom is alone. This is the mothering poem that doesn't. Mother. This is the card with love spelled a.b.o.v.e. Over now, the days of nursing in public, of baby powder like tear gas. There. That was the end of sappy. Of trees cut down. Of prime. Of odd numbers and integers. Your children as your least denominator. Your children as your common core. This is a teaching poem. This poem will not be graded. You are an A+. Of course, you will need to be signed and returned to someone by tomorrow.

How to Swing a Hammer

The house that Jane built doesn't have mold, but remnants
of other lives: skin cells in morning coffee, dead bugs,
a mason jar filled with broken vows.
The ghosts speak freely among themselves, leave notes
for the repairmen that have been called, yet never arrive.
Sometimes there is song. Not so much singing,
but a background refrain of pipes clanking,
fuel tanks running dry.
It all sounds like a nursery rhyme:
Don't leave me.
Don't leave me.
Could be the dead dog, could be the dead air,
could be the crows circling the cracked birdbath,
threatening
the pregnant calico,
the flock of songbirds fleeing her outstretched paw.

On Forbidding Certain Words at the Dinner Table

I have to tell you about the orange cat
asleep (not asleep) in the usual
position next to the neighbor's car.

Which is to say, dead. Eyes
open. Fur not warm, not cold, but wet.
The children want confirmation,
want the word for breathing.

Which is to say, is it really over?
Do you see his beating heart?
How do you spell *asphyxiation*?

Ask a mother this question and watch
the breath she has been holding,
up until this stormy June afternoon,
stream down her cheeks.

Mother: another word for stray.

Home: another word for white,
for spine like pearls, broken picket fence.

Family is another word.
Face in the dirt, don't scare the children.
Pretend you're still alive.

You read the dictionary,
but find few words
for *splintered, shattered or vows.*

Lolling head of the family,
you and the dismembered doll
legless, armless, naked on the lawn,
staring at, not seeing, that cat.

Animals should never
leave their bodies by way
of the neighbor's careless steering.

Leave bad driving to the mother
with no license, no registration.

Love as Sunfish with Hook in its Eye

All that they mistook you for will tie your gut in a slipknot. Aren't you the girl who can wake things from the dead? Aren't you a magic carpet? A magic key to a magic cave in a land smelling of fresh baked bread and nutmeg? Which is to say, after you were a mother, they thought your pussy was golden, thought it smelled like home. Then they swore the lock was broken. To them you were a kitchen with the oven always on. Once, they mistook you for a strand of DNA uncoiled, one thousand times more slender than the fishing line they used to snag and snare. If only you hadn't mistaken them for catch and release, for carry in/carry out, for *Only You Can Prevent Forest Fires*. You were their wise owl, as willing to walk across coals, as you were sure you could swallow the hook, spit it back out.

The Town Witch Tries to Make Friends

She offers her left arm,
her good arm,
her casting spells arm.
She opens

wide her perfect mouth
veils the sharp tips of her teeth
with a clean tongue,
speaks in the gibberish of women.

She promises not to eat their husbands
or handle their food,
dirty their laundry or covet their gardens.

As usual she has it all wrong.

As usual the men do not cooperate.
Three of them have offered to kiss her
behind their tool sheds,

in the back seats of their cars,
under cover of a new moon.
When you are not a wife,
but a witch

even your own shadow blushes
in your company,
prefers you enter through the backdoor,
rolls up the *Welcome* mat

should you mention stopping by.
Your name is always spelled wrong
or when it is carved into the base of a tree,
the kitchen knife it was carved with

always the dullest blade slipped
back into the drawer
when the real wife
is making dinner.

The House That Jane Built

If you say the word mother enough times it becomes other, becomes moth and udder, mouth and over. This is the boot that stepped on the porch. This is the porch that welcomed the mat. This is the weight of the pressure-treated threshold. All of these are dangerous. He made of you a country song. You were a chainsaw. You held his whiskey throat in your hands. You called the tree with your children's names in a heart, *Timber*. Or. You were the queen of all frozen days, and he was a dormant elm. Which is to say, this is the single breath that broke the dead deer's back. This is the song that sang *I love you* while you strapped ice claws on your feet, climbed his frozen trunk. This is the vase that sits empty on the hearth, that used to hold the fire. No flowers inside or out, just a rusty truck in the driveway and a cake made from cigarette butts and half-truths on the railing.

Thirteen Ways of Looking at Home
—*After Wallace Stevens*

I.
Among a skyline of dark windows,
breathing lights,
the eyes of the gentle giant.

II.
I was of three nests,
like a hobo, or a hummingbird:
my tiny house, my children, my home.

III.
The home pulsed in dinnertime's
dark. The oven, the lamps,
the table set.

IV.
A house is alone.
A mother, her children,
their fish and hermit crabs, cats and dog
are one.

V.
Home does not know which to prefer,
the flickering bulbs, or the frozen pipes.
The muddy welcome mat,
or the footprints inside.

VI.
One season, icicles bar the family like jailors.
In another, sun melts them like popsicles left out in July.
The home sits idly by, turning calendar pages.

VII.
O neighborhood mothers,
why do you imagine fresher paint, broader beams, more acres to mow?
Haven't you heard that size doesn't matter?

VIII.
I remember walking home.
No. I remember running.
Home was waiting.
Never hungry, just waiting.

IV.
Sometimes,
with binoculars, I watch people outside their homes.
I ask mine to marry me.

X.
The ratio is always changing:
mothers to children,
children to blankets,
home to home to home.

XI.
If you could have just one home.

XII.
Home is a warning.
Don't leave me without a last goodbye,
a key on a red ribbon, a wreath on the door.

XIII.
These are the things I cannot tell my home:
the windows closed tight from the truth,
the breathing lights that pulse and pulse.

Mary Writes an Ars Poetica

This poem will only bring you to tears
when sung to the tune of any song
you ever made love to, accompanied
by a mourning dove or a window-drunk fly.

This poem is about what you see,
about the bottom of last night's wine glass,
four petals left touching tips
circled up as though they died dancing.

No. At first glance, you see two
half-empty bottles of water,
a bottle of ketchup and one wine glass,
and ketchup left out overnight is not
romantic, just a sign of low class.

Now do what we all do:
ignore what is in front of you.
Focus on the dreamy and the deathly:
how flowers turn blood tinged
when left to dry in morning's redwine sun.
Wine glass as globe as world.

Don't let the white cat hopping on the table
looking for scraps (or his lack of a wheelbarrow)
distract you from that wine glass
with its off-kilter concentric circles.

Don't let the chorus of gorgeous birdsong
distract you. That titmouse still loves you.
He will return
and return—
siren song as destiny.

Of course, you see the wine drops as blood stains.
When you say blood, you mean
you have been doing it all wrong.

You are a moth, not a robin.
Your nest a broken globe,
your children hungry fledglings,
your wings too wet to fly.

Our Lady of Dark Mysteries

The old black dog knows to turn around three times, even when all you say is *lie*. O Mother of rapt attention. O Mistress of Bones and Trust. How we dig holes and have nothing to fill them with. How the nuts we gather and bury are forgotten, and still, we grow whole forests. This is blind trust. This is separated at birth, still holding hands. Vows not yet written, cells unmindful of the dangers of splitting. Trust that the skin holds. Trust that the skeleton will not burst into flames. Spontaneous combustion as death threat, as daydream, as champagne toast at midnight. Mary didn't name the beast, but she will brush his dusty fur and read with care the ancient story between his ribs. If you are honest with your suffering, you will wake to find a waterfall at the base of your bed, a sooty face hovering before you, a clean rag to wipe away the darkness.

When the dark things show up

you might be in your pajamas making coffee. You might be folding your dirty underwear or praying beneath the sharp needle of a cold shower. Solitude appears on your doorstep dressed in a cheap, white sheet, no eye holes. If you've never been exposed to dark things, well, you may be in for some trouble. They say if you never experience pain, you can never know joy. Joy is the hug. Pain is the scratch on the side of your face that came first. The dark things ask for a side of bacon. The dark things smear cold grease on your lips and call it gloss. It's not quite clear who kissed you first: the dark thing, the joy, the pain. Some god's triumvirate stole your keys and surprised you in the foyer. If you shoot one of them on the stairs before they enter your home, drag him inside, put a knife in his hand. You can call it self-defense.

One Doll's Epistle to Discontent

And it came to pass that one day God was angry at Barbie. As it turns out, she wasn't his lost pin up after all, she was his mother and he expected more from her. Disappointment leaked from the oil pan, from the underinflated tire, especially from the spidery edges of the tiny gouge in her windshield. Barbie failed to perform routine maintenance. Barbie failed to wash her high cheekbones daily. Barbie allowed eyes to grow on her potatoes. When the root vegetables turn on you. When the Ziplocs tear. When the water runs brown, and the mud is white with mold. You are not my mother. You are not my girlfriend. When God is mad, and your tow truck driver has a lip that curves like a back country road. If lug nut, then flat. If fan belt, then snap. *Your neck is so long*, she cried. *The better for all the things*, he answered.

Mary Looks at Real Estate

The shades are dropping from the lamps
the wires are flames in her walls,
but Mary knows it's not yet time for change.

That light bulb inside her mouth?
Speaking to her cheek

about wattage and filament,
true love and broken glass,

how necks not threaded properly
sometimes forget how to shine.

Do not bite down.
This is what the farmer said
when she opened to his rough palms
in the barn that dark night. She is not your Mary.

Not your apron,
your ballad,
your scarred candle with a scant wick.

When you tumble in the dryer
they call you Bearer of Bed Sheets and Linen.

Splayed across the mattress
you are The Blessed Vessel of Friction
and Release.

O Mother of the Oven,
O Queen of Flashlights and Headlamps.

When the rooms are empty
and the power cut off
does the tree falling through your window
make a sound?

Mary Kneels in the Garden

She is prepared for plants out of place,
weeds to follow.
Lady of the Dandelion.
 Mother of the Lion's Teeth.

The other women cultivate neat bushes,
grow showy
cacti on their front lawns.

To eat what is not meant to be eaten.
To swallow
 the hairy stem
  the jagged leaf.

Ask the woodpecker why she leaves
her nest,
why she gorges on ivy. She will tell you

about the beauty of the berry
the joy of running a tongue
over a living thing—thick, white, round.

Toxicodendron radicans.
Beware
the hairy arms,
 the hands with slim fingers,

the fine golden hairs. Poison as seasonal
danger, as lover vining your trunk,
creeping toward your throat.

Your obituary a record of children hidden
in a dying tree,
an urge to devour,
 a case of mistaken identity.

          You will never be the loud bird.
Make love to the worms,
the larvae and harmless seeds.
From your devastation, beauty.

Mary Pays Homage

The art of mothering isn't hard to master;
so many children filled with the intent
to be lost that their loss is no disaster.

So much depends
upon

a booster
seat

sitting on the roof
of an SUV

while a wrong-shoes-for-the-weather
mother

searches
for her keys and morning coffee.

When I say children, I mean
gingerbread house,
mean stepmother,
mean

artificial slate sidewalk
artfully arranged,
leading
to a front door with a wreath,
a witch inside making dinner.

Lose your family every day. Accept the fluster
of slamming doors, the mealtime badly spent.

Stand etherized before the crusted sink,
your hair a half-deserted streak behind you

while the children come and go
talking (each one) of the one that got away.

After the second glass of wine
you will know
what it is you plan to do
with your one wild and precious life.

After a fashion, the chickens will raise themselves,
will have sense enough
to come in out of the rain.

The Fireman's Daughter Extinguishes One More Fire

The ghosts walk into the kitchen and you cook them. No. Your grandmother and your mother walk into the Sunday kitchen and ask why you haven't waxed your floor. You wax poetic about bleach and flour and how salt puts out fires. The smoke from your oven is a shade, is your grandmother's white hair. You don't ask why. Your mother has widowed the mountains to visit you on the saddest day of the week. The bare bulb in the ceiling weeps lemon juice, the lamps in the empty living room have sold their gold. Your lover left you in the middle of the night. Now nothing glows, not even the oven's coiled arms. Is it true your grandmother rose from her grave beside the brook without a trace of dirt? Is it true your mother is not even dead yet? If pie, then man. You fold fear and three egg whites into a bowl of sugar each time you think you hear your lover whisper *meringue*.

Preparedness Checklist for Imminent Death

1. First, do not suppose this is a drill.
2. At all times, in any part of the day, do not be alone.
3. Consider a bodyguard, a lover, a chaperone.
4. Be loud at all times, unless you see death out of the corner of your eye. At that time, begin banging pots and pans, clapping wildly, whistling the French tune your father taught you.
5. After whistling, sing loudly. Death expects a big entrance.
6. *Alouette, gentille alouette. Alouette je te plumerai.*
7. As death approaches, wrap your hands around his neck. Death is all the men who have tried to kill you. Snap and pull the feathers. Death is a bird. If you are able, and you have not lost your strength, unlock death's skeleton. Arrange the pieces back inside your own unblemished skin. Death is the puzzle you have been working on for most of your mothering.
8. By now, you are winning.
9. By now, Mama, you find your heart beating a thousand times a minute, which is to say, you are a small bird and death is miles behind you. It is a myth that you have flown on the backs of larger, stronger animals. It is a myth that you need a checklist. Death was a bird, but you are the absence of bones. You are broad breast and flight, itch and preen.
10. When the pain in your head comes back, cradle it. Sing the broken vessel a lullaby.
11. *Je te plumerai la tête. Je te plumerai la tête. Et la tête. Je te plumerai les ailes. Je te plumerai les ailes. Et les ailes, et les ailes.*
12. The loss of your head and eyes will not make you a cadaver, a corpse, or a widow.
13. Your death will be less drill than myth. Someone will still try to fondle you. Your children will ask you for food. No one will believe you are gone, even as your feathers settle to the ground.

Jill Crammond was born and raised in the Adirondack mountains of New York State, and now resides in the suburbs of Albany, NY with her two children and an assortment of pets. She holds a Masters of English from The College of St. Rose. An early childhood educator, she teaches art and leads a band of tree-loving three-year-olds at a nature-based school. She is a medium and tarot reader and is currently studying to be a psychic detective.

Her poems have appeared in literary magazines and anthologies such as *Sweet Tree Review, Limp Wrist, Tinderbox Poetry Journal, Mom Egg Review, Pidgeonholes, Unbroken Journal, Mother Mary Comes to Me: A Pop Culture Poetry Anthology* (Madville Publishing), *Fiolet & Wing: An Anthology of Domestic Fabulist Poetry,* and *Fire on Her Tongue: An Anthology of Contemporary Women's Poetry* (Two Sylvias Press). Her work has been nominated for a Pushcart Prize, and her poems recently appeared as part of Poem Village, a community program celebrating local poetry in the Adirondack town of Saranac Lake.

www.ingramcontent.com/pod-product-compliance
Lightning Source LLC
Chambersburg PA
CBHW022126090426
42743CB00008B/1025